MY GYEONGJU
(SOUTH KOREA)
PHOTOGRAPH MEMOIR

DANIEL NARDINI

To order additional copies of this book, contact:
Xlibris
844-714-8691
www.Xlibris.com
Orders@Xlibris.com

ISBN: Softcover   979-8-3694-2311-0
               EBook   979-8-3694-2310-3

Print information available on the last page

Rev. date: 05/22/2024

Contents

Dedication

I wish to dedicate this book to my dear wife Jade, my best friend in South Korea Wang Sih Cheng, my good friend Bill Yoon, and my wife's family Jade's mother Lee Soon Won, her brother-in-law Giesig, and her sister Moon Son. I will always love and remember these wonderful people. I also wish to dedicate this book to the Malpass Library at Western Illinois University, my alma mater.

Remnants of an Ancient City

I worked at YBM/ELS from February of 1996 to March of 1997. During that time I lived in Seoul, and when I had vacation time I traveled throughout the country. One of my favorite places to visit was Gyeongju. Gyeongju is located in North Gyeongsang province, and has a current population of 264,091. The modern city of Gyeongju is not unlike other mid-sized South Korean cities that I have seen. A lot of the downtown area is made-up of non-descript modern two-story buildings, and the sidewalks are made of stone tiles that I have seen in other cities like Seoul and Incheon. Like so many modern South Korean cities, I got to Gyeongju by bus. South Korea has an excellent public bus system that goes to all major and minor cities throughout the country. Visitors can also reach Gyeongju by train. Unlike Seoul or Incheon, Gyeongju did not have narrow sidewalks. It was possible for people to ride bicycles on the sidewalks throughout much of the city. I saw many kids and even adults riding bicycles from place to place. There were also bicycle rental places in downtown Gyeongju for the purpose of traveling through the city by bicycle.

Probably the most distinguishing feature of Gyeongju is its ancient heritage. Most of Gyeongju is modern, but the remaining five or so percent is what makes the city totally different. As one goes outside the downtown area, you will find remnants of a very ancient past. Bases where columns used to stand that were part of Buddhist temple and palace complexes litter the rice fields. A lone stone pagoda stands in a rice field that once was part of a Buddhist temple. Gyeongju, once officially called Seorabeol in ancient times, was the capital of the Silla Kingdom. Founded in 57 BCE (Before the Current Era), the city was the capital of the Silla Kingdom until 668 CE (Current Era). From 668 to 935 CE, Gyeongju became the royal capital of the Unified Silla Kingdom when Silla unified for the first time the whole Korean peninsula under its rule. The current name of Gyeongju was given to the city in 940 CE by King Taejo of the newly established Goryeo Kingdom further north in the city of Gaesong. Gyeongju means "congratulatory district" in Korean. Under Silla, Gyeongju was a far larger city than it is today---believed to have been three to five times as large. Filled with homes of both the wealthy and commoners, Buddhist temples and palaces, and many royal monuments, Gyeongju suffered through destruction and neglect over the centuries as it became a small rural town. By a miracle, Gyeongju was spared the destruction of the Korean War (1950 to 1953). The North Koreans never advanced into Gyeongju, and hence Gyeongju remained in South Korean hands for the entire war.

The remnants and ruins of what past Gyeongju has now makes Gyeongju an open air museum. Indeed, archaeologists have carried out surveys and digs to uncover what the ancient city once possessed. A lot of what they have discovered is now on display in the Gyeongju National Museum. But there are some historic sites that still remain intact in one capacity or another. These original places are Tumuli Park, Bulguksa, Bunhwangsa Pagoda, and Cheomseongdae. These historic and cultural relics from the Silla Kingdom have survived the test of time, and are excellent examples of Silla's glorious past. I explored these places, and they were worth my time. These are remnants of an ancient city, and it is these places I wish to share.

Daniel Nardini
Chadwick, Illinois
2024

Bases that used to be columns for a Buddhist temple

Remnants of pillars and cross beams of a former temple

Close-up of a pillar showing a faded image of the Buddha

A lone pagoda in a rice field

Tumuli Park

Of all the historic sites in Gyeongju, Tumuli Park is one of the few located *in* downtown Gyeongju. This area is made up of large to very large hills that are in fact tombs of kings, queens and some nobles from the pre-unified Silla period of the First to Seventh centuries CE, to the Unified Silla Kingdom of the Seventh to Ninth centuries CE. There are a total of 23 such tombs in Tumuli (also called Daereungwon) Park. Those Silla tombs built in the later Unified Silla period are known, but those built from the First Century to the Sixth Century CE are largely unknown. This is not unusual because these tombs were built long before Buddhism came to the Silla Kingdom (Buddhism came to Silla between 527 and 535 CE), and hence we are not sure of the rulers or nobles who might be buried in these places. Since written records were not made consistently before the advent of Buddhism, we may never know the identities of those buried in some of these tombs. We only know that those buried in these tombs were once prominent people in the Silla. Incidentally, the practice of burying prominent people in a hill-like tomb has long been popular going way back into pre-history Korea, and even now South Koreans bury their dead in mountain cemeteries reserved for family members.

Because Tumuli Park is one of the few Silla sites that remain relatively intact, this area is a treasure trove of ancient Silla artifacts still lying undisturbed for centuries. Only one of these tombs was ever excavated, in 1973. This was Cheongmachang Tomb belonging to that of King Michu who lived in the Fifth Century CE. Among the discoveries in this tomb is the now famous painting of a mounted horse, and some of the now famous gold Silla crowns on display in the Gyeongju National Museum. The tomb yielded hundreds of gold, silver and bronze objects used in everyday life for the king as well as glass beads and the lacquer coffin he and his queen were sealed in. We can only guess what the other tombs might contain, but for now they remain sealed. Once the Silla Kingdom ceased to exist, this area became a backwater when succeeding ruling houses came to power. Whoever were buried in the earlier Silla tombs might have been forgotten even during the Unified Silla period (it must be remembered that the Silla Kingdom in its entirety lasted for 1,000 years).

As I walked along the designated foot path in the park, I always admired how this area has been a part of Korean history for 2,000 years. It thrilled me to be walking in the same footsteps that royals, nobles and even ordinary people of centuries ago once tread. What was the rest of the city like back in the days of the Silla? I could imagine it, but I will never know. I only know that today ordinary Koreans walk along this path of the park and see what their ancestors had built. They may not think twice about what this area really meant to their ancestors, but they do know that it is all a part of their long history.

The entrance to Tumuli Park

A tomb from the early Silla

One of the larger tomb mounds

The tomb of King Michu; the only one to be excavated in Tumuli Park

A walkway leading to a large tomb mound

One of the largest tomb mounds in Tumuli Park believed to be from the 1st Century CE

Another large tomb mound

King Michu's tomb from a distance

An unknown tomb mound from the 2ⁿᵈ Century CE

Bulguksa

After taking a bus and walking through a forest, I came to the front edifice of Bulguksa, one of the most famous sites in the Gyeongju area. What struck me about this Buddhist temple is how architecturally different it is from other Buddhist temples that were built in later periods. The front entrance into the temple complex is constructed of large square stones. The hand rails were also made of stone, and the roof of the front entrance was likewise grand in scale. Inside the temple complex are two well-known stone stupas (pagodas) called Dabotap and Seokgatap. These two stupas were originally from the Silla period, and by some miracle survived into the present day. Considering the rest of the temple complex had been left in ruins for centuries, it is amazing these two stupas were not destroyed. Even more amazing was the discovery in Seokgatap in 1966 of a bronze Buddha statue, silk clothing, and a woodblock print of Buddhist sutras. For 1,500 years no one had imagined that such treasures had been hidden in this stupa.

The individual temples were richly decorated with paintings, and flower motifs characteristic of Korean art can be found in Bulguksa like in other Buddhist temples. Surprisingly, there was an ancient stone lantern that is also from the Silla era like the stupas. I was not sure whether any of the Buddha statues were from the Silla period, but the temple complex had many beautifully made Buddha statues by master craftsmen as I had seen in other temples throughout South Korea. Bulguksa as we know it was first constructed between 751 and 774 CE. The temple was badly damaged during the Japanese invasion of Korea (also called the Imjin War) from 1592 to 1598. Towards the end of the 19th into the early 20th centuries Bulguksa was left in ruins. From 1969 to 1973, then South Korean President Park Chung-hee had the whole temple complex reconstructed to what it is today. President Park is remembered for restoring this part of Gyeongju's cultural heritage.

Bulguksa is owned by the Jogye Order of Korean Buddhism; the same order that owns Jogyesa in Seoul. Many visitors to the temple are also Buddhist adherents who desire to see this place as part of their traveling circuit to see temples of the Jogye Order. Bulguksa attracts all kinds of tourists from not only around South Korea but also from around the world to see this one magnificent piece of Silla architecture. I had visited this temple a couple of times when I was in Gyeongju, and likewise I enjoyed the Buddha in the Sokkuram Grotto that had been part of the Bulguksa grounds but had been "lost" for centuries until it was accidentally rediscovered in the early 20th Century. I always wondered if there might be other Buddha statues or other cultural relics in the mountain range surrounding Bulguksa waiting to be rediscovered?

The front entrance to Bulguksa Temple

All of the foundation stones are original

Two of the three entrances to Bulguksa

Bulguksa is the only surviving Buddhist temple from the Silla period

The main entrance into Bulguksa Temple

Dabotap Pagoda, believed to have been constructed in 751 CE

Seokgatap,like Dabotap, also built in the year 751 CE

A lantern shaped stone pagoda from the Silla period

A prayer hall

One of the living quarters for the monks

Another prayer hall

One of the oldest buildings at Bulguksa. Note the Silla architecture

Anapji Pond

When I first ventured to Anapji Pond, I found it a very serene place to relax and observe the lake and birds singing in the trees. There were five pavilions surrounding the lake, and some visitors walked along the length of the lake. I saw fish in the lake, and at times birds, usually cranes, bobbed for fish. The current Anapji Pond is a total reconstruction (not original) of what archaeologists believe the place might have looked like in the 7th Century CE. According to the oldest surviving record on Korean history, known as the **Samguk Sagi**, written in the year 1145 CE during the Goryeo Kingdom period (935 to 1392 CE), Silla King Munmu had Anapji Pond built for his amusement and relaxation. Archaeologists have uncovered remnants of a wall that had surrounded Anapji Pond, and a system of canals that fed into the pond.

Archaeologists also uncovered 33,000 objects that had been thrown into the pond. These objects included roof tiles of the former buildings that had stood on the site, bronze Buddha statues, jewelry, pottery, and many ordinary items used for personal hygiene. The last mention of Anapji Pond was again in the **Samguk Sagi** when Silla King Gyeongson held a royal reception there in 931 CE. No other mention is made of Anapji Pond, but during the dynastic wars fought in the declining years of Silla the capital was attacked and all of the pavilions and palaces near the pond were destroyed and what was not stolen was thrown into the pond. The pond itself decayed into ruin and was little more than a swamp. In 1974, as part of an effort by then South Korean President Park Ching-hee to restore the historic sites in Geyongju, Anapji Pond was reconstructed based on the archaeological evidence of what the place might have looked like.

Today, Anapji Pond is a tourist attraction like Tumuli Park. Located close to the center of downtown Gyeongju, it is within walking distance. Hence, it is possible to walk from Tumuli Park to Anapji Pond in the same day. Although not an original relic from the Silla period, the artifacts found in Anapji Pond nevertheless has helped South Korean archaeologists to know what both royalty and the common people had used during that time period. In that respect, Anapji Pond is an important heritage site in Gyeongju.

The entrance to Anapji Pond

Part of the pond next to the pavilion

Anapji Pond during the fall

A scenic view of Anapji Pond

Bunhwangsa Pagoda

Seemingly out of place amid the rice fields today, Bunhwangsa Pagoda was once part of Bunhwangsa Temple that had covered the whole area. That whole temple complex is long since gone, and only this pagoda remains. I saw remnants of what used to be temple foundation stones in the ground as well as some stone pillars with Buddhist carvings on them that were once the part of Bunhwangsa Temple. The pagoda, constructed of black andesite rock, once stood in Silla times at nine stories. Today, only three stories remain. The pagoda was once an important shrine in the Silla capital. Records mention the pagoda as part of the larger Bunhwangsa Temple complex that covered several acres of the capital. There were four main temples in the temple complex, and Bunhwangsa Temple was used during special occasions in prayer for the Buddha's intercession during times of trouble.

The pagoda itself we know was built in 634 CE on the instruction of then Silla Queen Seondeok. Over the centuries, the pagoda stories collapsed until only the three stories remain. The inside of the pagoda, which was originally hollow, was covered with the debris of the original six floors that had collapsed. In 1915, a Japanese colonial archaeological team (remember, Japan had taken over Korea as a colony in 1910), did some work on the pagoda. They cleared out the inside of it, and discovered a relic box with the remains of an unknown Buddhist priest, gold and stone relics, and coins and Buddha statues that may have been stored in the pagoda for centuries. These objects are now on display in the Gyeongju National Museum. Although now prevented by stone blocks, there were passageways into the pagoda. Each passageway is guarded by guardians from Korean folklore.

Like Gyeongju, the pagoda was spared from the ravages of the Korean War. The Bunhwangsa Pagoda was declared a national treasure by the South Korean government in 1962, and has been visited by both South Korean and foreign tourists for decades. Next to the pagoda is a well where the temple once drew its water from.

Frontal view of Bunhwangsa Pagoda

The pagoda is surrounded by lions in each four directions

Another lion at the end of the four square base of the pagoda

Two guardians to one of the four entrances into the pagoda

The former temple well, now capped, that served Bunhwangsa Temple

Cheomseongdae

In Tumuli Park, where the most prominent people from the Silla period are buried, is a magnificent stone structure like almost no other in South Korea or anywhere else in the world. This round stone structure is called Cheomseongdae, and is unique because it was used as an ancient observatory. Built on order by Silla Queen Seondeok when she was a princess in the 7th Century CE, Cheomseongdae was created for the express purpose of making seasonal observations of the heavens and the climate changes. This was very important because the scholars who observed the seasons through Cheomseongdae could note the weather patterns to help the farmers for the upcoming growing season and also of any possible severe winters. Such calendar observations were crucial for the survival of the Silla Kingdom because an observation miscalculation could mean a bad harvest.

Cheomseongdae is one of the oldest if not the oldest observatory created in the ancient world still standing. We know what its purpose was because from surviving Silla record fragments as well as later accounts. Scholars during the Silla would climb up Cheomseongdae by ladder to peer into a square hole in the shape of a Chinese character meaning "well." The light going into the structure was almost like an ancient telescope which could help plot the heavens and star alignments. This was very advanced for the time period, and it is possible that there might have been more such structures created in the Silla Kingdom for the same purpose. We only know that Cheomseongdae is the only one which has survived and has survived pretty much as it is for the past 1,300 years.

Today, Cheomseongdae is one of the surviving monuments from the Silla Kingdom. Despite the wars, rise and fall of other ruling houses after Silla, and the ravages of time, Cheomseongdae comes to us from the distant past. This observatory is a remnant of the sciences that once existed in the Silla Kingdom. We may never know what other technology Silla may have had since those records that may have existed did not survive. In the case of Cheomseongdae, we fortunately know that in this case the Silla Kingdom had some quite advanced scientific technology which made Silla a great civilization that has been mentioned well beyond Korea's border in ancient times.

The ancient observatory Cheomseongdae in Tumuli Park

Cheomseingdae, made of approximately 365 stones (all of the days of the year), used by the Silla Kingdom for calendar observations

This is one of the few intact surviving monuments from the Silla period

Buddhism at the Heart of Gyeongju

Since Buddhism was introduced to the Silla Kingdom in the 6th Century CE, it had played a prominent part in helping to maintain a unified Silla state. Buddhism was the state religion, so it enjoyed patronage from the Silla royal court. Buddhist monasteries were set up all throughout the kingdom, and with it a unified network of communications. Messages from one end of the country to the other were relayed by couriers who were supplied with food and water from the temples, and Buddhist monks also served as scribes at the Silla court as well as in local government administrations. Some of the most learned people in Silla were Buddhist monks, priests and nuns. They learned to read and write Chinese characters and help to write sacred Buddhist scriptures that would help foster learning in the country.

Buddhism helped to foster the arts and architecture especially in the Unified Silla Kingdom. A lot of the artwork that is available in the Gyeongju National Museum and other museums in South Korea were created during the unified period. The beautiful bronze, silver and gold statues that I saw in the National Museum of Korea in Seoul were created during the Silla. Those Silla tombs from the unified period that had been excavated showed considerably more wealth than those before the Unified Silla time. We are not entirely sure what the architecture of Silla's palaces and other structures might have been like (although they were heavily influenced by Chinese architecture), but we know from the surviving temples we see today like Bulguksa that Buddhism had a very powerful impact on Silla architecture.

And it was because of Unified Silla that Korea became a unified country for the first time. Gyeongju became the capital of this unified new state, and when the Goryeo Kingdom was founded, it took a lot of what Silla had created and took it all to what became Goryeo's capital Gaesong in today's North Korea. Goryeo copied Silla's bureaucracy, architecture, and had proclaimed Buddhism as the state religion. Like the majority of people in Asia, Koreans follow the Mahayana branch of Buddhism, and the Koreans were instrumental in spreading Buddhism to Japan. In fact, Buddhism still plays a major role in Gyeongju to this day. Besides tourism and people going to Gyeongju for religious instruction in Buddhism, there is Uidok University which was founded in 1995, and is owned and operated by the Jingkak Buddhist Order. Ever since Buddhism was introduced to the Silla Kingdom, Buddhism has been and remains an important part of the city of Gyeongju.

Printed in the United States
by Baker & Taylor Publisher Services